THE GREAT OUTDOORS

by Cath Jones and Mónica de Rivas

THE GREAT OUTDOORS

CONTENTS

Chapter 1	Going Away	4
Chapter 2	The Den	10
Chapter 3	The Raft Challenge	18
Chapter 4	A Tall Tree	24

CHAPTER 1
GOING AWAY

"It's here!" Red jumped out of his seat and pointed at the large coach which had just pulled up outside the school gates. He slung his backpack over his shoulders and joined the scramble to line-up.

There was a buzz of excitement as the class boarded the coach. Within minutes, everyone was belted in. The engine rumbled into life and the doors slid shut.

At last they were on their way to Queen's Wood Adventure Centre. Red felt like he'd been waiting for this all year. Three whole nights away from Mum! Could school trips really be as good as the other kids said? Beside him, Stacey giggled. "Are we there yet?" she asked.

"We've only just left!" Red checked his watch. He knew it would be at least an hour before they arrived because Dad had shown him where they were going on a map. Whenever they went away camping together, Dad always insisted on plotting out the route with him.

Red pulled out a piece of paper from his bag. An hour was more than enough time to make an origami dragon. He began to fold the paper.

From the seat behind came a snigger.

"Weirdo paper folder," muttered a voice.

Red didn't need to turn around to know it was Jack. From experience, he knew that reacting was the worst thing he could do. He concentrated on his origami dragon, folding the paper carefully and ignoring Jack.

Stacey cast a mean look over her shoulder before tugging on the sleeve of Red's fleece. "What are you making?" she whispered.

Red held up the folded piece of paper. "This one is going to be a sort of half-dragon peacock."

They sat in companionable silence for the rest of the journey, Stacey reading her book and Red engrossed with his origami. While he folded the paper, he thought about the days ahead. He was sure that lots of the activities would be things he'd already done with Dad. It was going to be great fun.

CHAPTER 2
THE DEN

Within an hour of arriving at Queen's Wood Adventure Centre, Red was standing in the middle of a shady wood.

A young woman clapped her hands and an expectant hush fell.

"Good morning class. I'm Susmita, your activity leader. Are we ready for our first challenge?" she asked.

"Yes!" yelled the class.

Susmita gestured around the wood. "You see all those sticks and bits of rope and netting lying around? Use them! You have one hour to construct a waterproof den."

Red smiled to himself. Building a den was going to be easy. He thought of all the times he and Dad had built shelters in the woods. Wild camping in secret places was incredible. Red smiled to himself as he remembered the marshmallows he and Dad had toasted on the camp fire the weekend before. They had tasted delicious.

It didn't take long for Stacey and Red to gather enough large sticks to form the centre of their structure.

"We need a net to cover it," Red said.

Stacey nodded. "I've seen one." And she dashed away to fetch it.

Red formed six large sticks into a tepee shape and wound rope around the top. He pushed down on it, just as Dad had shown him, to test its strength. It held firm. Red smiled with satisfaction. Suddenly, Red heard someone approaching behind him.

"Lost your bits of paper?" hissed a voice.

Red's heart sank. He didn't need to look round to know who it was.

"I've come to show you how to build a proper den," Jack said as he barged past.

Red edged away as Jack piled up sticks on top of the tepee. *Where was Stacey, Red wondered?* It seemed like ages since she'd dashed away to find a net. He crouched down in the shade of an enormous oak tree. He pulled out a sheet of paper and began to fold, focusing on each careful crease. His mind drifted away from Jack and the den.

After a while, Stacey appeared pulling a huge net along the ground. She stopped when she saw Jack.

"We don't need that," Jack sneered. "We're not going fishing."

Stacey ignored him and crouched next to Red. She peered at the latest origami creation.

"It's a peacock," he said and held it out on the palm of his hand. "Would you like it?"

Stacey grinned. "Thanks."

Eventually, Jack pronounced the den finished. Red stared at the pile of sticks. It didn't look as good as one of Dad's dens, he thought.

Suddenly Susmita appeared. "Good effort, guys. Now, are you ready for the water test? Is your den waterproof?"

Red shrugged.

"Of course," said Jack, confidently. He sprawled inside the den leaving no room for anyone else.

Susmita tipped up a watering can.

"Hey!" Jack sprang out of the den, his hair dripping wet.

CHAPTER 3
THE RAFT CHALLENGE

Red stood by the side of the swimming pool, listening to Susmita. He was sure the next task would be fun if only Jack didn't interfere again.

Susmita pointed to some empty water containers. "This afternoon, you're going to build a raft," she said. "You can use anything around the pool, for example you could tie these containers together."
She clapped her hands enthusiastically. "Remember, I'll be watching you all. In particular, we're looking for good teamwork. Ready-steady-go-guys!"

Stacey charged across the poolside, grabbed four containers and flung each of them towards Red. "Hurry up!" she urged. She picked up a large net and some rope and held them up questioningly.

Red nodded and began to lash the containers together using knots Dad had taught him. Stacey fixed the net over the top of the whole raft.

From the other side of the pool, Susmita suddenly bellowed, "Good teamwork, guys! But will it hold your weight?"

Stacey began to drag their raft into the water.

Red hesitated for a moment. He spotted Jack tying together some planks of wood. At least he's too busy to bother with me, he thought.

Stacey gave the raft a shove and it plunged into the water. "It floats!" she exclaimed with delight. She grabbed Red by the hand and they tumbled onto the raft, sending a mini tidal wave sweeping across the pool. For a moment, the raft sank beneath the water before bobbing up and down precariously.

Stacey let out a loud, satisfied whoop. Lying on their stomachs they began to paddle with their hands. Suddenly, Stacey sat up. "Have you got any origami animals left? We could use one as a figurehead."

Red pulled a crumpled paper dragon out of his pocket and propped it on the front of the raft. "Perfect!" Stacey laughed.

Suddenly, there was a loud shout and another raft bashed into theirs. They tipped to one side and the dragon slid into the water.

"Oops!" Jack sneered.

Stacey glared at him. It was the last straw. "Why don't you just leave Red alone?" she blurted out angrily.

Jack smirked and paddled away. Red sighed as he watched the dragon float off.

CHAPTER 4
A TALL TREE

"Your final challenge involves tree climbing," announced Susmita. She pointed up. "Can you retrieve a flag from the tree?"

Red's heart raced with excitement. Tree climbing! He remebered how proud he had been when he'd watched his dad win the Fastest Tree Climber competition last month, for the third year in a row. Now it was Red's chance to be like his dad.

Stacey high-fived Red. "This'll be a piece of cake!"

But before they could start climbing, Jack barged past. "I'm going first." He was almost half-way up the tree when he slipped, letting out a loud shriek.

"I think Jack is stuck," Stacey announced loudly.

Susmita peered up. Jack had his arms wrapped around the main tree trunk in a tight hug. His eyes were closed.

"Are you okay?" Susmita called.

There was no reply.

Red gazed up at Jack. Someone needs to rescue him, he thought, and I'm the best climber. He stepped up to the tree and began to move effortlessly up. As he climbed, he could hear his dad's calm voice in his head, encouraging him.

Finally Red reached Jack. Jack's face was white and his breathing was panicky. Red perched on a branch. He took out his last sheet of paper and began to fold.

"Everyone's good at different things, Jack," he said in a quiet voice. "I do origami and I climb trees, just like my dad. I can teach you to climb trees if you want."

After a moment, Jack opened his eyes. For a few minutes, he watched Red's fingers quietly twisting and folding. Gradually, Jack's body relaxed and his breathing calmed.

"Do you want to climb down with me?" Red asked.

Jack grunted and nodded his head.

"Watch where I put my feet and what I hold onto," Red instructed. "If you copy what I do you'll be okay."

"I'll try," murmured Jack.

Red breathed in the smell of the damp leaves around them and let out a happy sigh. He began to lead the way.

At the bottom of the tree, Jack stood with his hands thrust deep in his pockets. He stared at his feet.

"You were brilliant," Stacey mouthed at Red.

Jack looked at Red. "Thanks," he mumbled.

"I said you'd be okay," Red said.

Jack shrugged his shoulders. "Sorry," he muttered. "You know, for everything …" His voice trailed off. Then he reached into his backpack and pulled out an expensive-looking pad of paper. He held it out. "Would you like this? You know, to fold?"

Red smiled. "Thanks."

"Maybe you could show me how to build a waterproof den too?" Jack grinned as he spoke.

"Okay," said Red. He turned to Stacey. "The three of us could build an amazing den!"

Things to think about

1. What sort of mood is Red in at the start of the story? How does he feel about the school trip?
2. Why do you think Jack gives Red a hard time?
3. Why do each of the tasks go wrong?
4. What makes Jack realise he needs Red's help?
5. How do Stacey, Red and Jack each learn about the value of teamwork in the story?

Write it yourself

This story is based on what it is like to overcome bullying, and to learn to work as a team. Think about a story based around the need for teamwork.

Plan your story before you begin to write it.

Start off with a story map:

- a beginning to introduce the characters and where and when your story is set (the setting);
- a problem which the main characters will need to fix in the story;
- an ending where the problems are resolved.

Get writing! Think about characters with different personalities and how each one may have to adapt or change in order to get along together. Make sure you include a resolution.

Notes for parents and carers

Independent reading
The aim of independent reading is to read this book with ease. This series is designed to provide an opportunity for your child to read for pleasure and enjoyment. These notes are written for you to help your child make the most of this book.

About the book
Red is excited about his school trip away to an adventure centre. But he soon encounters trouble from Jack in his class, who seems determined to wreck any challenge. Soon Jack realises he needs Red's help and discovers the meaning and value of teamwork.

Before reading
Ask your child why they have selected this book. Look at the title and blurb together. What do they think it will be about? Do they think they will like it?

During reading
Encourage your child to read independently. If they get stuck on a longer word, remind them that they can find syllable chunks that can be sounded out from left to right. They can also read on in the sentence and think about what would make sense.

After reading
Support comprehension by talking about the story. What happened? Then help your child think about the messages in the book that go beyond the story, using the questions on the page opposite. Give your child a chance to respond to the story, asking:
Did you enjoy the story and why? Who was your favourite character? What was your favourite part? What did you expect to happen at the end?

Franklin Watts
First published in Great Britain in 2019
by The Watts Publishing Group

Copyright © The Watts Publishing Group 2019
All rights reserved.

Series Editors: Jackie Hamley and Melanie Palmer
Series Advisors: Dr Sue Bodman and Glen Franklin
Series Designer: Peter Scoulding

A CIP catalogue record for this book is
available from the British Library.

ISBN 978 1 4451 6523 3 (hbk)
ISBN 978 1 4451 6524 0 (pbk)
ISBN 978 1 4451 6946 0 (library ebook)

Printed in China

Franklin Watts
An imprint of
Hachette Children's Group
Part of The Watts Publishing Group
Carmelite House
50 Victoria Embankment
London EC4Y 0DZ

An Hachette UK Company
www.hachette.co.uk

www.franklinwatts.co.uk